# IT'S TIME TO EAT CREAM PIE

# It's Time to Eat CREAM PIE

## Walter the Educator

Silent King Books
A WhichHead Entertainment Imprint

Copyright © 2024 by Walter the Educator

All rights reserved. No part of this book may be reproduced in any manner whatsoever without written per- mission except in the case of brief quotations embodied in critical articles and reviews.

First Printing, 2024

Disclaimer

This book is a literary work; the story is not about specific persons, locations, situations, and/or circumstances unless mentioned in a historical context. Any resemblance to real persons, locations, situations, and/or circumstances is coincidental. This book is for entertainment and informational purposes only. The author and publisher offer this information without warranties expressed or implied. No matter the grounds, neither the author nor the publisher will be accountable for any losses, injuries, or other damages caused by the reader's use of this book. The use of this book acknowledges an understanding and acceptance of this disclaimer.

It's Time to Eat CREAM PIE is a collectible early learning book by Walter the Educator suitable for all ages belonging to Walter the Educator's Time to Eat Book Series. Collect more books at WaltertheEducator.com

**USE THE EXTRA SPACE TO TAKE NOTES AND DOCUMENT YOUR MEMORIES**

# CREAM PIE

Oh, look at the pie, it's creamy and sweet,

# It's Time to Eat
# Cream Pie

A dessert so special, it's time to eat!

With a crust so golden, and fluffy white,

It's the perfect treat for our delight.

The whipped cream swirls like clouds so high,

Topped with love, oh, my, oh, my!

Underneath, a filling so smooth,

Every bite will make us groove.

Banana, chocolate, or coconut, too,

Each kind of cream pie is fun to chew.

The flavors melt like a happy dream,

Oh, what joy in this tasty theme!

Grab your spoon, it's time to dig in,

Let the cream pie adventure begin!

A little bite here, a big bite there,

It's a dessert that's beyond compare.

# It's Time to Eat
# Cream Pie

The crust is crumbly, oh, so fine,

With every taste, it's simply divine.

A little sweet, a little tart,

This creamy pie warms every heart.

Sharing slices with family and friends,

The happiness just never ends.

"Thank you, pie!" we all agree,

You're the best dessert for you and me.

One bite, two bites, and then a cheer,

"Cream pie is the treat we hold dear!"

Every spoonful brings a smile,

A dessert that's always worth the while.

When the last bite's gone, we'll say with a sigh,

"Oh, how we love that creamy pie!"

It fills our hearts with sugary glee,

## It's Time to Eat

# Cream Pie

The best dessert there'll ever be.

So next time you see that pie on a plate,

Don't hesitate, it's time to celebrate!

With every bite, it's joy and fun,

Cream pie's a treat for everyone!

Now let's clap and give a hooray,

For cream pie time makes the perfect day.

Whether coconut, chocolate, or banana so sweet,

# It's Time to Eat
# Cream Pie

It's always time for cream pie to eat!

# ABOUT THE CREATOR

Walter the Educator is one of the pseudonyms for Walter Anderson. Formally educated in Chemistry, Business, and Education, he is an educator, an author, a diverse entrepreneur, and he is the son of a disabled war veteran. "Walter the Educator" shares his time between educating and creating. He holds interests and owns several creative projects that entertain, enlighten, enhance, and educate, hoping to inspire and motivate you. Follow, find new works, and stay up to date with Walter the Educator™ at WaltertheEducator.com

www.ingramcontent.com/pod-product-compliance
Lightning Source LLC
LaVergne TN
LVHW052011060526
838201LV00059B/3976